My First
Hidden Picture
Coloring Book

by

Lynn Adams

DOVER PUBLICATIONS, INC.
New York

Published in Canada by General Publishing Company, Ltd., 30 Lesmill Road, Don Mills, Toronto, Ontario.

Published in the United Kingdom by Constable and Company, Ltd., 3 The Lanchesters, 162–164 Fulham Palace Road, London W6 9ER.

My First Hidden Picture Coloring Book is a new work, first published by Dover Publications, Inc., in 1993.

International Standard Book Number: 0-486-27478-0

Manufactured in the United States of America
Dover Publications, Inc., 31 East 2nd Street, Mineola, N.Y. 11501

Note

This book contains 48 pictures in which there are hidden elements that you have to find. They include letters of the alphabet, numbers, animals and household items. The captions beneath the pictures tell you what to look for. Once you have carefully examined and found everything in a picture, you can check your answers in the Solutions section that begins on page 53. But the fun doesn't end there. You can also color all the drawings, making the hidden objects stand out or keeping them concealed so that you can test your friends.

A bell, a mouse, a heart, a seal and **a bird** are hidden
somewhere in this underwater scene.

4

Can you find **a shoe, a candle, a baseball bat, a screw-driver, a jug** and **a rolling pin** concealed among the rushes of Danny the duckling's favorite pond?

Judy's cat just adores ice cream. While he eats, can you locate **a shell, a bell, a shoe** and **the letters G, T** and **C** hidden here?

It's that apple-picking time of year again. But can you
pick out **a palm tree, a fishhook, an ice-cream bar, a
comb, a pig** and **a teapot?**

Somewhere on Billy's space suit are **the numbers 4, 5, 2, 3** and **7.**

Susan is telling a wonderful bedtime story. But you don't have time to listen: **a cup, a kite, a shoe, a sock, a lollipop** and **a sailboat** have got to be found here.

Little does Captain Jamie suspect **the acorn, the trumpet, the key, the mushroom, the flower** and **the pliers** concealed amid the clouds and the sea, and even aboard ship.

10

The letters P, L, V, N, C, Y and **J** must be sought in this picture of George, a most musical cat.

While Katy plays on her swing, you too can have fun seeking out **a bird, a rabbit, a heart, a cup, a tortoise** and **a spoon.**

A pair of scissors, a woolen hat and **the letters E, V, Q, J** and **H** have to be discovered in this picture of Angela riding her bicycle.

13

Brian the bear is an expert flipper of pancakes. But he will need your help to find **the saucepan, the toothbrush, the book, the apple, the cane** and **the pencil** hidden in his kitchen.

14

"Apple pie is my favorite dessert," says Freddy the cat. Can you discover **the banana, the sailboat, the dog, the cat** and **the rabbit** before Freddy's pie gets cold?

Joe is out playing in the autumn leaves, but he hasn't noticed **the bird, the spoon, the frog, the bunny's face, the fish** and **the pear** hidden among them.

These two mice are playing hide-and-seek in the broom. But **a cap, a pair of pants, an umbrella, a baseball bat, a hammer** and **a screwdriver** are hiding there too. Can you see them?

It's bedtime for this tired bunny. Can you find **the letters V, Y, L** and **C, a shoe** and **an arrow** in this picture before your bedtime?

Two lollipops, an apple, a feather and **a light bulb** haven't caught the eye of this scuba-diving puppy.

Timmy and his dog are so busy flying their new kite that they just haven't noticed **the sailboat, the pear, the clothespin, the star, the anchor** and **the bunny's face** hidden here.

Can you discover **the mitten, the tortoise, the moon, the bird, the musical note** and **the pencil** in this picture of Sarah and her colorful rag doll?

Danny is having fun building sand castles. Can you help him find **a rocket, a snail, a fork, a sheep, a fishhook** and **a polar bear** before the tide comes in?

A heart, a candle, a star, an arrow and **a feather** need to be found in this picture of Johnny, who has his hands full with a box of frolicsome kittens.

While Katrina hangs the washing out to dry, you can stay busy looking for **a bell, a fish, a hammer, a snail, a trowel** and **a bird** in this picture.

Toby is reading all about his favorite subject—bones.
But **the letters A, V, L, J** and **T** have disappeared. Can
you find them?

A flower, a comb, a bird, a feather, a mouse and **a moon** are quite out of place in this snowy scene.

"All aboard!" cries Gus the engine driver, as he gets up steam. Can you locate **a book, a cup, a frying pan** and **the numbers 5, 6, 7** and **8** before the train moves off?

A mushroom, a butterfly, a hammer, a wristwatch and **a trowel** are lurking somewhere in this picture. Where are they?

Lizzy wants to be a dancer when she grows up. While she practices, you'll have your hands full looking for **an umbrella, an ice-cream bar** and **the letters W, X and Y** hidden here.

29

It will soon be time for supper for this pair of hungry mice. But first they need your help to find **the banana, the mitten, the cat, the snail, the moon** and **the sail-boat** hidden in their kitchen.

What a sleepy puppy! He has no idea that **a pair of scissors, a jug** and **the letters U, V, Z** and **Y** are hidden around his kennel.

Oh dear! Poor Barney is in trouble with an angry bee who wants his honey back. While Barney makes his escape, you can look for **the cup, the two birds, the whale, the carrot, the cat** and **the frog** hidden here.

A bunny's face, a sheep, a woolen hat, a paintbrush, a heart and **the number 7** have to be discovered in this picture of Mary and Jill enjoying their tea in the garden.

33

Climbing trees is what these two kittens like best. But this tree is different. It is concealing **a spoon, a football, a bird, a candle, a tortoise** and **a boot.**

The letters A, B, C, N, V, E and **J** are waiting to be uncovered in this picture of a cuddly young acrobat.

Just look at that frog splashing around on the lily pads! But don't forget to search for the hidden objects: **a pair of pliers, a mouse, a butterfly, the numbers 2 and 3,** and **the letter L.**

Are your eyes sharp enough to find **the bunny's face, the cat, the feather, the saucepan, the needle, the rabbit** and **the paintbrush** hidden in this peaceful scene?

Spring-cleaning has got to be done. But there's more to be tidied than first meets the eye. Where are **the two fish, the banana, the lollipop, the bird** and **the bell?**

Strumming away on his guitar, this musical frog will need some help finding **the spoon, the cane, the fork, the trowel, the carrot** and **the duck** hidden here.

"Oops!" exclaims Ruby, almost losing her balance. While she gets her breath back, look for **the pretzel, the clothespin, the lollipop, the safety pin, the light bulb** and **the thumbtack.**

Michael has only one ice cream to share between himself and two hungry cats. Let's hope no one misses out. But don't you miss out on **the paintbrush, the acorn, the whale, the rabbit** and **the swan** in this picture.

What could be better than a snooze beneath a shady toadstool? Well how about finding **an acorn, a spoon, a fish, a duck, a cup** and **a songbird?**

Even with his glasses on, old Herbert the mouse can't see **the duckling, the songbird** and **the letters J, W, U** and **i** hidden around him. Can you?

This sleepy kitten certainly isn't fishing for **the butterfly, the rabbit, the two ducks** and **the songbird** hidden in this picture. Can you do a better job?

It's soapsuds galore for this puppy. But there are also **the letters C, E, L, D, O, F, J** and **i** to be found.

Some cats love to take a nap in the afternoon. But this one is missing all the fun of finding **the house, the seal, the sailboat, the carrot** and **the mouse** hidden here.

A cup, a paintbrush, two ducks, a rabbit and **a shoe**
must be sought in this wintry landscape.

This bear is just too busy painting lovely pictures to notice that he's surrounded by some strange hidden objects: **a shoe, a duck, a sailboat, a saucepan** and **a musical note.**

In this picture of David on his rocking horse are hidden **a palm tree, a seal, an anchor, a horseshoe, a banana** and **a frog.**

Rupert the rabbit is tucked in very cozily. While he sleeps, you can seek. Look for **a toothbrush, an acorn, a rolling pin, a pair of scissors, a heart** and **a sailboat.**

Sally and her kitten may be looking over the garden fence, but they haven't seen **the jug, the bird, the mouse, the feather, the shoe, the bunny's face** and **the star** hidden here. Can you see them?

Solutions

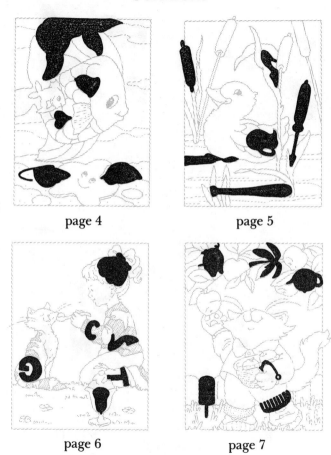

page 4

page 5

page 6

page 7

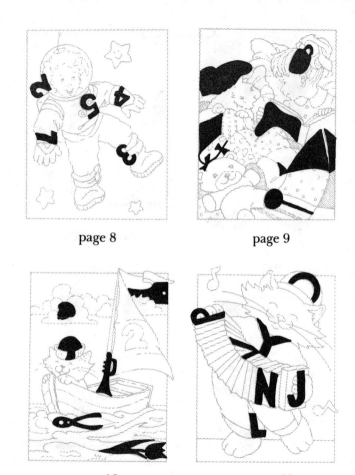

page 8

page 9

page 10

page 11

page 12

page 13

page 14

page 15

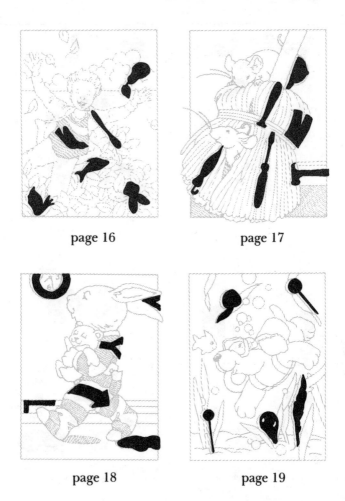

page 16

page 17

page 18

page 19

page 20

page 21

page 22

page 23

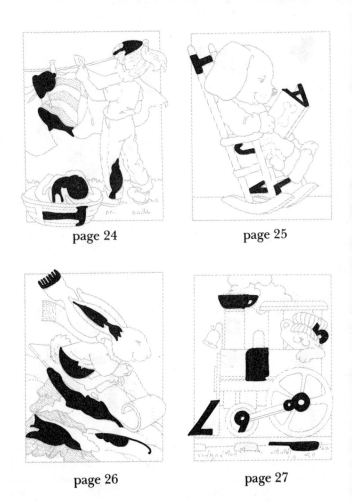

page 24

page 25

page 26

page 27

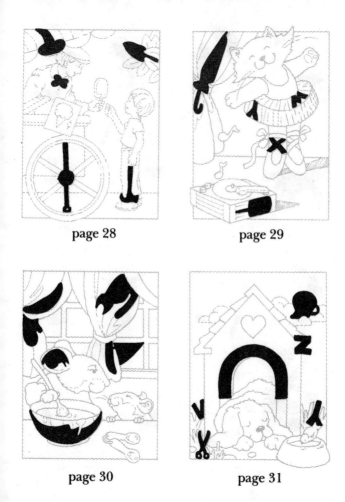

page 28

page 29

page 30

page 31

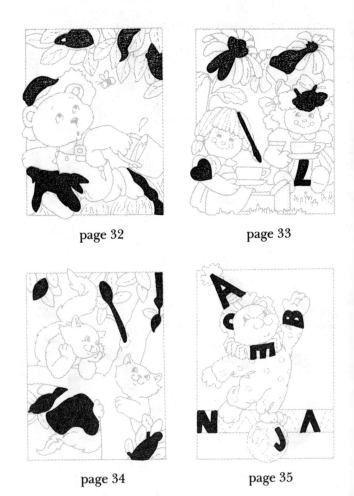

page 32

page 33

page 34

page 35

page 36

page 37

page 38

page 39

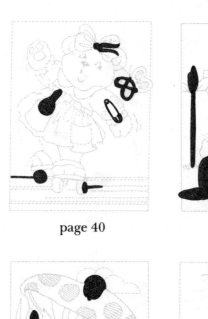

page 40

page 41

page 42

page 43

page 44

page 45

page 46

page 47

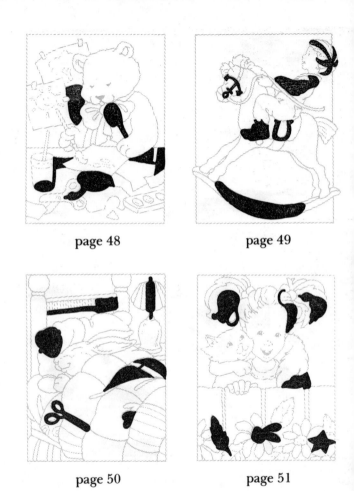

page 48

page 49

page 50

page 51